PARTNERS IN THE PROCESS

The Formation of Deacons' Wives

Karen A. Harmeyer
Maria Thompson MacLaughlin

One Liguori Drive
Liguori MO 63057-9999

Imprimi Potest:
Thomas Picton, C.Ss.R.
Provincial, Denver Province
The Redemptorists

Imprimatur:
Most Reverend Robert J. Hermann
Auxiliary Bishop
Archdiocese of St. Louis

ISBN 0-7648-1290-4
Library of Congress Catalog Card Number: 2005924103

© 2005, Karen A. Harmeyer and Maria Thompson MacLanghlin
Printed in the United States of America
05 06 07 08 09 5 4 3 2 1

All rights reserved. No part of this book may be reproduced, stored in a retrieval system, or transmitted without the written permission of Liguori Publications.

Scripture quotations are from the *New Revised Standard Version of the Bible*, © 1989 by the Division of Christian Education of the National Council of the Churches of Christ in the USA. Used by permission. All rights reserved.

Liguori Publications, a nonprofit corporation, is an apostolate of the Redemptorists. To learn more about the Redemptorists, visit Redemptorists.com.

To order, call 1-800-325-9521
www.liguori.org

For the deacons' wives, the deacons, and their families—each person, each family unit, teaches us what life and relationships are all about.

For my darling Matthew, who made me a deacon's wife, and my family, whom I love more than life itself.

CONTENTS

INTRODUCTION vii

THE BEGINNING 1
    The Call 3
    The Decision 8

THOUGHTS ON BECOMING A DEACON'S WIFE 11
    Stormy Beginnings 13
    Spousal Expectations and Relationships 16
    Relationship Models 18
    When You Don't Feel Called to Be a Deacon's Wife 23
    Reflections of an Older Wife 29
    Embracing Change 33
    Networking 36
    Theological-Reflection Groups 39

FAMILY MATTERS 41
    Children 43
    Finances 46
    Health Issues 49
    Pastor-Deacon-Family Relationships 51
    Time Management 56

AN ENDING AND A BEGINNING 59
    Lifestyle Changes 61
    Ordination 68
    A New Life 74

EPILOGUE 81

ADDITIONAL RESOURCES 85

INTRODUCTION

The call to the diaconate is not a "couple thing." It's a man thing, a husband thing, a thing from which the Roman Catholic Church has expressly eliminated women. This issue has forced many wives to do a lot of soul-searching when their husbands say they want to become deacons.

Forty-eight wives came together a little over five years ago when the Diocese of Richmond, Virginia, started its first diaconate-formation group. We were diverse in the beginning—different education levels, different ages, different lifestyles—but today we are a cohesive group who went through the formation period with our husbands and are living lives as deacons' wives in the Church community.

All diaconate-formation programs are not the same; all are open only to men, but in most other respects there is little consistency among them. Some are two-year, some are four-year, and some are five-year programs. Some offer graduate-level college credits, others do not. Some require wives to participate in almost every aspect of the training, others do not. The experiences of deacon-candidates' wives differ as much as the diaconate programs.

What we have tried to do, therefore, is present the challenges and rewards we experienced when our husbands underwent formation training. In addition, we include the stories of other wives in our group as well as composite experiences as seen through Karen's eyes.

As our deacon-candidate husbands studied and prayed, we prayed that the deacon decision was sound. We prayed that our husbands would find the right fit for their skills and talents. We prayed that what God envisioned for each deacon and his family would come to be.

This small book is our gift to future deacons' wives, wherever they are and whatever type of program they find themselves in. We believe that our path in writing this book was led by the Holy Spirit, and we hope you receive as many blessings in reading these pages as we have received while writing them.

Karen A. Harmeyer
Maria Thompson MacLaughlin

THE BEGINNING

*I will tell you what wisdom is
    and how she came to be,
and I will hide no secrets from you,
but I will trace her course from the beginning
    of creation,
and make knowledge of her clear,
and I will not pass by the truth.*

THE WISDOM OF SOLOMON 6:22

THE CALL

Karen A. Harmeyer

My name is Karen Harmeyer. My husband, Gary, and I are a military couple, serious about our national commitment, serious about our family commitments, and serious about our relationship with God.

Gary was first asked to become a deacon in the early 1990s by Father James Merold while we were stationed at Naval Hospital Great Lakes, Illinois, about 30 miles north of Chicago. Gary and I discussed the effect that becoming a deacon would have on our relationship and family, but before we reached any conclusions, the Gulf War intervened. With Gary supervising operating room services at Naval Hospital Great Lakes and working on a mobile surgical team and me the Nurse Corps Officer on the executive staff of the Naval Reserve Readiness Command, our military obligations overrode the question of the deacon call. After the war, Gary received orders to Naval Medical Center Portsmouth, Virginia, where our family entered the next phase of consideration for the diaconate.

We joined St. Luke Catholic Church, a small parish of

a little over 200 families. Gary readily became a member of the parish council and parish nursing ministries and eventually became the parish assistant. One day Father Gene, the pastor, encouraged Gary to attend an information meeting for men interested in becoming deacons. Gary asked me to go with him. He needed my support at this session and at future sessions should he decide to enter the program.

The primary speaker, Father John, talked about the role of a deacon: to minister to the poor, sick, and untended; give Communion; serve as lector and coordinator; assist or officiate at liturgical celebrations and in sacramental preparation; and perform internal and external parish outreach activities.

Father John said that Bishop Sullivan envisioned a four-year graduate-level preparation somewhat at the master's level. Negotiations were taking place with Saint Meinrad School of Theology in St. Meinrad, Indiana, to have faculty flown to Richmond once a month for Friday night and all-day Saturday classes. The academic sessions would be rigorous and comprehensive. The curriculum would demand voluminous reading, active discussion, studying, writing papers, and testing. Daily prayer was essential.

Wives were expected to attend the monthly class sessions and would receive credit as students if they chose to do the course work and take the tests. Wives' attendance at weekend sessions was mandatory during the first year and encouraged for the remaining three years; the diocese did not want marriages to suffer by focusing on the deacon candidate alone.

One man who said that his wife had a new business and would not be able to attend the weekend sessions was told not to consider becoming a deacon. It was obvious that conflicting priorities between spouses, employment issues, family tragedies that would pull the deacon and his wife temporarily or permanently out of ministry, and differing views of the importance of family, church, other commitments, and the separate lives of married couples would be ongoing issues during the four-year formation period.

The Diocese of Richmond's application process, which would take at least three to six months, included a mandatory interview for the deacon candidate and his wife before a panel of deacons, priests, religious, and laypersons as well as a psychological evaluation and a criminal background check at the candidate's expense.

I asked what criteria would be used to determine whether the applicant was accepted or rejected. A tense moment followed as Father John pointed his finger at me from across the room. I could almost feel the point of his finger pounding on my sternum. "What is your agenda?" he shot back.

I said I believed that good decisions were based on data and criteria and repeated my question in a neutral tone. A diocesan staff member in the back of the room introduced himself as a member of the diocesan marriage tribunal and said that all of the information would be gathered and assessed for its total content, the implication being that a candidate would be accepted unless he were a criminal or were overwhelmingly unable to attend the formation sessions and perform the duties of a deacon.

The most important thing I learned at the information session was that Gary truly felt a call to become a deacon and that my support would be essential to the process. I could not yet envision myself holding hands with and standing beside a man wearing a Roman collar. However, I was willing to do so because this man is my husband, the father of our children. I love this man. I support this man in uniform, in jeans, or in a Roman collar.

For they will be made holy who
  observe holy things in holiness,
and those who have been taught
  them will find a defense.
Therefore set your desire on my words;
long for them, and you will be instructed.

THE WISDOM OF SOLOMON 6:10-11

THE DECISION

Karen A. Harmeyer

Gary and I used the following guidelines to reach our decision to begin the diaconate application process:

- Understand that a deacon candidate spends much time studying, writing, attending class, participating in discussions, going on retreats, and praying at least every morning and evening. Balancing family demands with quickly escalating deacon demands will be a constant struggle.

- Listen and share your thoughts and feelings as you grow personally and spiritually. The ripening and maturing processes will challenge all family members and relationships.

- Include family members in decisions that affect them and continually reassure them of their value.

- Seek guidance from clergy members and religious leaders. Share your highs and lows, challenges and successes. Learn from them and share your gifts with them.

- Do research so you are able to make informed decisions about undertaking deacon formation training and following through with ordination.

- Evaluate your lifestyle, employment status, and ability to say yes when obedience overrules reason as the guiding principle in making decisions.

- Pray together, at least daily, that you make good decisions by listening to the wisdom and strength acquired through prayer.

Thoughts on Becoming a Deacon's Wife

*I learned without guile and I impart
without grudging;
I do not hide her wealth,
for it is an unfailing treasure for mortals;
those who get it obtain friendship with God,
commended for the gifts that come from
instruction.*

THE WISDOM OF SOLOMON 7:13-14

STORMY BEGINNINGS

Karen A. Harmeyer

When faced with a man's call to become a deacon, his wife experiences feelings alien to her normal day-to-day emotions. Initially, I was not excited about the prospect. In over 30 years of marriage, I have had to repeatedly acknowledge that I am not number one in Gary's life. Early in our marriage we were still in nursing school, and time devoted to study, clinical practicum, and passing nursing boards took precedence. Once in the Navy, our careers sapped time and energy. Then children took front stage, then military relocations and school-related activities. When Gary retired, I encouraged him to take some time off before taking a civilian job. That was when the diaconate program came into our lives.

How did I feel about his becoming a deacon? I felt set aside. It was my turn to be Gary's primary focus; if he became a deacon, it would never happen. Because of my lack of enthusiasm, he felt unsupported and that our marriage was on shaky ground. Gary suggested consulting a marriage counselor to sort things out, and I agreed.

One session was all it took to affirm that our marriage was still on solid ground and to convince Gary that I stood beside him. I was still not enthused about being relegated to second place, but I resigned myself to a wait-and-see approach.

The deacon candidates were also sorting through feelings and decisions. Gary and I participated in a memorable discussion in which the men shared that if it hadn't been for their wives, they would have probably become priests. The conversation was lively as the men talked about their near-miss with the priesthood. As one after another of the men agreed, and as each exaggerated on the theme, they spoke about falling in love. They went on to describe how hormones affected their decision-making.

First, my eyes glazed over. Then they blazed. "Enough," I said in a low, clear voice. "This is nonsense. You are all demeaning the value I place on my marriage vows. You each chose to marry, for whatever reason. We, the wives, did not snatch you away from your calling to the priesthood. You were called to be married; you chose to follow that call. Don't blame it on hormones or the woman you chose to spend your life with. You chose to enter the sacrament of marriage and celebrate it every day of your life. Let's put a little reason into this discussion."

They all agreed. They had been called to marriage, not plucked just before sailing off into the sunset to become a priest which, from the initial tone of their voices, they considered to be a higher calling. I'm certain there were some lively discussions after everyone went home that evening.

When I enter my house, I shall find rest
   with her;
for companionship with her has no bitterness,
and life with her has no pain,
   but gladness and joy.
When I considered these things inwardly,
and pondered in my heart
that in kinship with wisdom there is
   immortality,
and in friendship with her, pure delight,
and in the labors of her hands,
   unfailing wealth,
and in the experience of her company,
   understanding,
and renown in sharing her words,
I went about seeking how to get her for myself.

THE WISDOM OF SOLOMON 8:16-18

SPOUSAL EXPECTATIONS AND RELATIONSHIPS

Karen A. Harmeyer

One Saturday morning, I overheard someone say, "On Friday afternoons, couples rush to get here on time. They've prepared for this session by studying, praying, and arranging to be gone for a weekend. They noisily gather for the evening prayer service and enthusiastically participate. Even though they're tired and stressed, they attend the Friday evening classes without complaint. At 9:30 PM they are ready for class to be finished, and they go off on their own for the rest of the night.

"A miracle happens overnight, because when they arrive in the morning, they are glowing and content. They are somewhat sleep deprived, yet renewed in spirit and energy. One of the gifts they receive on the weekend is time to be with each other. This is why the wives *must* attend the weekend sessions. They are feeding their relationship." This miracle happened every formation weekend.

Some of the deacon-formation couples were very

eager for the monthly getaway weekends to begin. Certainly they fussed about the hotel expense, arrangements for the care of children and other family members. But as a working woman with teens at home, I jumped at the prospect of having Gary all to myself for one whole weekend every month.

Some couples did face challenges in finding childcare, and occasionally they had to bring their children with them. The folks in charge of the formation sessions also helped arrange on-site childcare. But most of the couples preferred to have the time away while their children slept in their own beds, ate their own food, and followed their other familiar routines. And when you're physically out of reach, it's harder to be disturbed.

The couples who lived close enough to drive back and forth from weekend sessions faced some of the greatest challenges because their families, employers, and parishioners had physical access to them, especially after they got home on Friday nights and before they left for Saturday morning sessions.

RELATIONSHIP MODELS

Karen A. Harmeyer

Most of the wives I encountered during the four-year formation period fell into one of the following five categories:

1. Wife as handmaiden and caretaker of the deacon

A church-conceived, paternalistic model in which the wife is a handmaiden responsible for feeding, clothing, and caring for the deacon and everyone else. She goes where he goes and provides support in whatever form the deacon requires. She may carry his vestments and keeps inventory of his albs, stoles, and clerical shirts. Her ministry is supporting the deacon in his ministries. She is always in the background.

2. Two-for-the-price-of-one minister couple

The deacon and his wife are equal partners in the ministry, with the deacon's duties and responsibilities divided between them somewhat equally. The parish perceives them as one unit with two personalities.

3. Life of my own; life of his own

Each person selects a ministry. Each person contributes unique talents and efforts in his or her own personal way.

4. I'll participate sometimes, but I refuse to be at church every night

In this picture of reluctant participation, the deacon is busy with ministry. The wife may siphon some of her time from other priorities to contribute to ministries, but she will not hang around the church just because her husband is there. She knows that being in the same place and doing shared activities does not equate to quality time together.

5. Balance of ministry, marriage/family, and job

Balance is established between the priorities of married life: each other, ministries, family, job, and civic duties.

No matter which of these relationship models is adopted by the deacon and his wife, the importance of a spiritual life as a couple cannot be underestimated. During their wedding ceremony, the marriage partners affirm the presence of God in their relationship. Each shared day and experience is a threesome, with the spiritual element enhancing and enriching the relationship. This theme continues and heightens when the couple undergo the deacon-formation process.

The planners of the Diocese of Richmond diaconate program decided that wives were a vital element of the process, so class attendance by both spouses was mandatory for the first year. The deacon candidates were required to seek a spiritual advisor, and the wives were encouraged to do so as well. The implied goal was that marriages should not suffer because of the deacon training. In truth, the mandate was probably not necessary since most wives understood that this new direction would implicate, obligate, and sometimes dictate their involvement. Mutual and simultaneous spiritual growth of the marriage partners is a powerful image of a sacramental marriage: if each marriage partner grows simultaneously in intimacy as a result of the gifts of a rich spiritual life, the gifts grow exponentially.

Here are some guidelines for recognizing spousal expectations and achieving balance in the relationship:

- Establish boundaries to allow time and energy for the relationship as well as the ministry.

- Set up personal boundaries without coercion or external influence.

- Encourage open communication and negotiation.

- Keep romance alive and let marital love spill over from the home setting to others in your ministry.

- Let the joy of ministry enhance spousal and family interactions.

- Commit to prayer time together in addition to individual prayer and service attendance.
- Strive for balance in marriage, family, ministry, and other priorities.
- Foster openness and growth by using a spiritual advisor as a stimulus and facilitator.

*And if anyone longs for wide experience,
she knows the things of old, and infers the
    things to come;
she understands turns of speech and the
    solutions of riddles;
she has foreknowledge of signs and wonders
and of the outcome of seasons and times.
Therefore I determined to take her
    to live with me,
knowing that she would give me good counsel
and encouragement in cares and grief.*

THE WISDOM OF SOLOMON 8:8-9

WHEN YOU DON'T FEEL CALLED TO BE A DEACON'S WIFE

Robin S. McLane

If your husband is called to be a deacon but you don't feel called to be a deacon's wife, this is for you.

I am Protestant and raised our children in the Methodist church because my husband did not practice his faith during that part of our marriage. When he started going back to church, I felt as though I had to choose between supporting him in his spiritual growth as a Catholic and continuing to participate in the Christian fellowship that my children and I were comfortable with in the Methodist church. Because he knew I was struggling with his newfound passion for Catholicism, he didn't share his investigation of the diaconate program with me.

When he did tell me about it, I thought he had lost his mind. How could he imagine having time to take classes on weekends when he was working full time? Plus, we had two children, one with special needs. And when I found out I would also have to commit to attending classes with him the first year, I was indignant. I couldn't imagine him making the sacrifice to attend my graduate classes in education. How could he expect me to make the equivalent sacrifice? Anger and resentment dominated my emotions.

Despite my reservations, he didn't change his mind about applying for the program. When the time came for our interview as a couple, I just wanted to get through it without revealing the negativity I was feeling. I managed to hold it together through most of the questions. However, one member of the interview team—a gentle, wise nun—looked into my soul and said, "Tell us how you really feel." The floodgates opened. My husband was devastated. I was so embarrassed to have not only let him down, but to have let God down as well.

There were understandable concerns about our suitability for the program, and we were called back for a second interview several weeks later. By the grace of God, I calmed down and we sailed through this one thanks to our children, who had come along to be interviewed as well. Their support for their father came through with enough strength to overshadow my doubts.

The four years of the diaconate program were a roller coaster ride for me. The initial anger and resentment were somewhat balanced by the excitement of meeting new people. Some of the classes stretched me mentally and spiritually. We had been so involved with raising our children that we had not taken time just for ourselves, and I began to look forward to the weekends away with my husband.

The diaconate program forced us to focus on each other and on our spirituality. The car rides to and from classes became a time for discussion which, even when argumentative, helped me work through the negative feelings and doubts. We began to pray together and have devotions in the evenings—something new for us as a couple. The benefits of these activities, plus the new patience I saw in my husband as a result of his spiritual growth, helped our marriage grow in a way I could not have anticipated.

It took several years for the anger and negativity to completely dissipate. Just when I thought I had made major strides, the negative energy would well up inside of me and explode. Now I see that perhaps God was using me to test my husband's commitment to this program, but at the time I just felt guilty about my attitude because most of the other wives were actively involved and excited about being a deacon's wife. I, on the other hand, was scared of what would be expected of me when he was finally ordained.

God does not call all deacon's wives to fill a certain job description. My own ministries—working with youth at the Methodist church where our children were still involved and activities centered on my teaching profession—don't fit with my deacon husband's focus on liturgical responsibilities at the Catholic church. He has always encouraged my spiritual growth and my own avenues of expressing and pursuing it. We are a model of an ecumenical family who serve the Lord and worship in a variety of ways. It pleases me that people do not look down on my husband because his family is not as visible in the Catholic Church as they might expect.

My husband is called to be a deacon. I support him through prayer and service to God. Although it has been a long, uphill road for me, being a deacon's wife has challenged me and motivated my own personal growth. I thank God for that opportunity.

Here are some things I learned through the process:

- If God is truly calling your husband, nothing you can say or do will stand in the way. He may delay his answer, but it will eventually happen.

- Take one day at a time. When you look at the whole program and the responsibilities afterward, it is too overwhelming.

- Pray, give yourself time, be honest about your feelings, and don't be hard on yourself if you're not feeling excited about the changes occurring as a result of your husband's calling.

- Talk to a friend, relative, or even a counselor who can objectively listen and provide feedback to let you know that your feelings are valid and that you're not a bad person for having them.

- Don't try to make yourself into what you think a deacon's wife is supposed to be. Ask your husband to talk to other deacons whose wives assume a supportive but less traditional role.

- Network with a small group of candidates' wives.
- As a couple, we made the most progress on overnight retreats with our small theological reflection group. Discussions at home can get heated and go in circles.
- Treat yourself to a special activity together during diaconate weekends.
- God's plans are often very hard to perceive when you are in the middle of them. Have faith that God knows what's best.

*I loved her more than health and beauty,
and I chose to have her rather than light,
because her radiance never ceases.
All good things come to me along with her,
and in her hands uncounted wealth.
I rejoiced in them all, because wisdom
    leads them;
but I did not know that she was their mother.*

THE WISDOM OF SOLOMON 7:10-12

REFLECTIONS OF AN OLDER WIFE

Joan Jennings

The process was different for my husband and me than for many of the other older candidates, most of whom were retired. Walter was old enough to retire but had continued working for the State of Virginia as a school dentist because he loved the children and loved helping them. This full-time work situation stressed us as the travel, diaconate homework, and many other requirements accumulated.

I felt more alone than you would believe. Prior to our decision to pursue the deacon training, I had elected to stop working as a registered nurse by retiring early. Now my husband was either working or studying. There was little time left for us to visit our four grown sons and other relatives. There was no time to just have fun together.

God directed us to serve in a town approximately one hour away by car, which was considered adjacent by rural standards. This community welcomed us with open arms to their church and its small mission in yet another town.

We were fast developing a new set of friends. Every time we saw them, it was a marvelous experience. Although my new friends helped fill a void, I still felt lonely, but I didn't say much about this to my husband. I tried to be as supportive as I could be and even typed papers and helped with research. But I still felt that, even though I was learning a great deal, I was not finding fulfillment.

I was accustomed to having my husband go with me when I did my favorite things like going to see the Tennessee Lady Vols play basketball or visiting my elderly parents. I found that I needed to bite the bullet and go by myself when my father had surgery in Florida. Later, I made the long trip to Knoxville to see the basketball games alone. I never thought I could do this without Walter, but I did. I found my way there alone and even spent the night without incident. This was hard for a small-town lady who always had her husband to help her find the way.

The pressure of trying to make things easy for my husband so he could get enough rest and keep up his studies tended to pull us apart. I felt distressed over this, but I made up my mind that the diaconate was what he wanted to do. I needed to give him space, to find a hobby or something that I wanted to do to keep myself busy. I gave myself permission to try new things and be more adventurous. So, at the age of 63, I decided to pursue an old dream—to learn to ride a motorcycle. Walter thought that I was crazy but agreed that I should try. He encouraged me by offering to buy me a motorcycle if I passed the course, which I did.

In a way, this experience has given me a glimpse of how hard it has been for him to make a change by becoming a deacon. I made it more difficult by hanging on for the ride. My new attitude has allowed my husband to follow the Lord in the life he wants without my dependence weighing him down.

Yes, we were chosen or, to rephrase, Walter was chosen and I was blessed by being with him.

Because the whole world before you
*   is like a speck that tips the scales,*
and like a drop of morning dew
*   that falls on the ground.*

The Wisdom of Solomon 11:22

EMBRACING CHANGE

Karen A. Harmeyer

Knowing that as a deacon-candidate's wife you will be alone a lot does not make it easier, but you will see that it does have its advantages. Being alone allows you more time to structure activities to your liking. It may be a time to do something you never tried before, like learning to ride a motorcycle. Perhaps it is time to go back to college and seek that next academic level that was put off by marriage, child-rearing, or employment. Here are some other ideas:

- Make a to-do list of all the things you want to do that you never took time for in the past, such as a new hobby, exercise plan, creative art, or other imaginative activity.

- Make a things-I-would-really-like-to-have list and then figure out how to get them, fix them, adapt them, or cross them off if you decide you don't really want them anymore.

- Meet new people *and talk about more than the weather.*

- Expand your scope of interests and interactions by volunteering for causes and activities that you support and those you know nothing about.

- Travel, visit family members, go somewhere and do something new, or go on that trip that you postponed earlier in your life—alone or with friends.

- Pray more, read more, sing more, love more, share more, exercise more, and savor more.

*Therefore I prayed, and understanding was
    given me;
I called on God, and the spirit of wisdom
    came to me.
I preferred her to scepters and thrones,
and I accounted wealth as nothing
    in comparison with her.
Neither did I liken to her any priceless gem,
because all gold is but a little sand in her sight,
and silver will be accounted as clay before her.*

THE WISDOM OF SOLOMON 7:7-9

NETWORKING

Maria Thompson MacLaughlin

No one can deny that being an ordained deacon is an awesome responsibility; however, wives are the basic support system behind their husbands. They should be equipped with as much information as possible in order to ensure long-term success in the ministry to which they have also been called.

At the beginning of the program we discovered that, although each monthly deacon weekend allowed adequate time to get to know the other couples, it didn't allow enough time to increase the depth of friendship beyond the superficial. A turning point took place when technology was introduced. One of the candidates began e-mailing the other candidates, spreading the word about deaths, births, marriages, illnesses, and other news. With each message, we grew closer to the other candidates.

As time progressed, the e-mails grew to include schedule changes, reminders about papers, and more information about individual candidates. No one started an e-mail program for the wives, so we were dependent on our husbands for news about the other candidates. The husbands were becoming more familiar with each other in a short amount of time, but the wives were not getting to know each other.

The following activities would help increase networking between wives:

- Have get-acquainted sessions for the candidates' wives while husbands are occupied in class.

- Put together a directory of e-mail addresses and phone numbers to allow easy communication between wives. The directory could also include personal and professional information about the wives.

- Start an e-mail chain to share personal news as well as information related to the diaconate program. Ideally, one person would serve as the central contact.

- Schedule spiritual-reflection sessions for the wives as well as the candidates.

- Offer informational sessions for the wives. Being the wife of a deacon presents special challenges, and being prepared will bring comfort.

Although she is but one, she can do all things,
and while remaining in herself, she renews all things;
in every generation she passes into holy souls
and makes them friends of God, and prophets;
for God loves nothing so much as the person who lives with wisdom.
She is more beautiful than the sun,
and excels every constellation of the stars.
Compared with the light she is found to be superior,
for it is succeeded by the night,
but against wisdom evil does not prevail.

THE WISDOM OF SOLOMON 7:27-30

THEOLOGICAL-REFLECTION GROUPS

Maria Thompson MacLaughlin

From the onset of classes, groups of program participants who lived near each other met monthly to keep up the momentum established in class and to provide a nurturing environment for the candidate and his wife within the context of faith and spiritual issues in a smaller-group setting. Meeting places rotated from month to month to allow each couple to host the group.

Each session was primarily aimed at the needs of the candidate but sometimes included input from the wife. During the course of deacon formation, each group was asked to attend an annual overnight retreat where sharing, reflection, and Scripture would be uninterrupted by worldly responsibilities. These overnight theological-reflection retreats were usually held in a secluded atmosphere to eliminate distractions. During these annual retreats, a senior permanent deacon and his wife would plan the activities, while segments of the prayer sessions and scriptural-analysis time would be the responsibility of designated couples. Most of the group members attended these sessions because they were planned so far in advance that everyone could keep the date open.

The annual theological-reflection retreats allocated quiet time for couples to reflect on Scripture passages with one another; walks around the grounds promoted a more open atmosphere. And although they were structured, the weekends provided a chance to keep in touch with colleagues and to feel a sense of security in the ministry.

Having smaller-group gatherings improved bonding at the larger deacon-weekend gatherings because everyone felt a sense of belonging—including the wives.

The richness of small theological-reflection groups can be enhanced in the following ways:

- Create an environment in which the agenda, whether formal or informal, provides for spiritual growth and nurturance for everyone, not just the candidates.

- Encourage diverse speakers and presentations to broaden perspectives.

- Alternate planned agendas with free sharing time for variety.

- Provide time and tolerance for opposing views.

- Learn from each other as all participants grow spiritually.

Family Matters

I also am mortal, like everyone else,
a descendant of the first-formed child of earth;
and in the womb of a mother I was molded into
   flesh,
within the period of ten months,
   compacted with blood,
from the seed of a man and the
   pleasure of marriage.
And when I was born, I began to breathe
   the common air,
and fell upon the kindred earth;
my first sound was a cry, as is true of all.
I was nursed with care in swaddling cloths.

THE WISDOM OF SOLOMON 7:1-4

CHILDREN

Karen A. Harmeyer

We started diaconate formation with one daughter newly graduated from college and joining the Navy, two sons in their last year of college, one son in his second year of college, and a daughter still in high school.

One evening we gathered as many family members as possible to have an open discussion of our children's concerns about the diaconate program. What would this mean to them and how would it affect their lives?

Our oldest child, an adult, was primarily concerned about the toll that diaconate demands would take on our marriage. All five children wanted to retain the father-child time they currently enjoyed. They worried that as Gary became busier with studies and ministerial work, time for them would become less or that the time together would have to be scheduled early and enforced strictly. They also wondered whether they would be forced to modify their dress and behavior, spend more time in church, clean up their language, watch their alcohol consumption, and conform to other adult expectations. They had no desire to become angelic because of image impositions placed on them as the deacon's children.

Then there was the issue of deacon-formation weekends. Would our teenagers get into trouble in our absence? Probably. Would they get into trouble if we were there? Probably. But they would learn to handle life's little emergencies, such as fender benders, needing a ride somewhere at the last minute, and not having enough cash to cover a necessary expense. The increased independence they would develop would undoubtedly help them for the rest of their lives, and that would be a good thing for everyone.

Gary and I decided to focus on these points:

- Make a special effort to devote time to the children individually and as a group as Gary became more involved in studies and ministries.

- Always have time for their phone calls and e mail messages.

- Acknowledge their positive church involvement and church behaviors.

- Always take their concerns seriously and answer honestly when asked a question.

- Pray often as a family for strength and the wisdom to make the right choices.

...the beginning and end and middle of times,
the alternations of the solstices and the changes
    of the seasons,
the cycles of the year and the constellations
    of the stars,
the natures of animals and the tempers
    of wild animals,
the powers of spirits and the thoughts
    of human beings,
the varieties of plants and the virtues of roots;
I learned both what is secret and
    what is manifest,
for wisdom, the fashioner of all things,
    taught me.

THE WISDOM OF SOLOMON 7:18-22

FINANCES

Karen A. Harmeyer

In almost all cases, deacon candidates perform their ministries in addition to their primary employment. Life does not take a vacation while a deacon candidate undergoes formation. He must continue to contribute to the financial support of his family, and many times he is the sole source of his family's income. Our group of roughly fifty deacons-in-the-making was composed of a broad spectrum of professions and occupations. The largest group was in the healthcare field, but there were also teachers, engineers, and retired military-service members.

One of the deacon candidates in our group was unemployed. He wanted a full-time staff position at a parish and a salary that would allow him to support his family. Some parishes would like to provide this level of salary for full-time or part-time ministry, but church structure and the diaconate do not support this.

When the husband elects to become a deacon, he must realize that his clerical position will usually provide little to no income while demanding time and energy at all hours of the day and night. If he is semiretired or fully retired and in no need of extra income, this isn't as big an issue as it is if he will need to continue to work full-time. Some of the deacon couples had serious career choices and modifications to make as the husband added the role of deacon into the family equation. These are the points they kept in mind:

- Their families need shelter and food.
- Contracts with employers and clients must be honored until they expire or are severed.

*...nor will I travel in the company of
    sickly envy,
for envy does not associate with wisdom.
The multitude of the wise is the salvation
    of the world,
and a sensible king is the stability of any people.
Therefore be instructed by my words, and you
    will profit.*

THE WISDOM OF SOLOMON 6:23-25

HEALTH ISSUES

Karen A. Harmeyer

The four-year training period spanned a time with many health and emotional crises for the families undergoing the formation process. At least five people required significant medical attention. Given the average age of 55 years, this was not a surprise. Stress and mental illness also took its toll. During our formation period, the deaths of a deacon candidate and a permanent deacon who had served as mentor and spiritual advisor to many affected all of us deeply. We prayed for the ability to respond to a crisis and to recover from it.

Many deacon-formation couples and their families experienced the death of a parent during the four-year formation period. Many became caregivers for elderly or seriously ill parents, thus further taxing their reserve energy and family resources. Many accepted elderly relatives into their homes and served as caregiver twenty-four hours per day, seven days a week. The emotional toll of these situations stretched the limits of the candidates and affected their ability to carry out their other obligations.

She glorifies her noble birth by living with God,
and the Lord of all loves her.
For she is an initiate in the knowledge of God,
and an associate in his works.
If riches are a desirable possession in life,
what is richer than wisdom, the active cause
 of all things?
And if understanding is effective,
who more than she is fashioner of what exists?

THE WISDOM OF SOLOMON 8:3-6

PASTOR-DEACON-FAMILY RELATIONSHIPS

Karen A. Harmeyer

My husband once told me, "Don't let your family be the reason you decide not to do something. Look for the real reason and you will find that it is usually *yourself*." One day I met a furniture salesman who was a perfect example of this. He said he had left an active Protestant ministry because his congregation's demand, in his words, that he attend to their needs at all hours of the day and night, had taken its toll. While he was away, his children went to their mother for permission slips, lunch money, doctor's appointments, bedtime stories, and advice.

I asked whether he were still married. He nodded, but not in a very positive manner. All four children were either in college or working, and he didn't hear from them very often. He said that the congregation was thriving in spite of his absence.

I asked, "Why did your family feel so alienated from you?"

He said, "They thought I spent all my time at church and that I didn't want to be with them. I did it for them. It wasn't my fault. I did these things for them. I really did love them. I didn't *want* to get up at night to tend to other people's needs. I was just doing my work, my ministry, tending to my flock. I wanted my family to look up to me."

I think the problem was that he chose to be away from his family so that *others* would look up to him. He did everything for his own gratification and didn't notice its impact on his other relationships. After our conversation, I wondered whether Gary and the other deacon candidates were taking ownership of their relationships with their priests and congregations.

Many deacon candidates have a congenial professional relationship with their priests, and that relationship extends to the deacon's family. Pastors must relate to deacons and their families individually and within their limitations, and deacon candidates must find a way to balance their time and energy with their pastors' expectations.

However, not all deacon-priest relationships are collaborative. One wife wrote to me that she and her husband were dealing with "priestly jealousy, [which] seems to stem from guidelines set by the diocese in allowing deacons to be self-supporting, married men as well as ordained ministers. Publicly it appears we have the support of our pastor but…we have been ostracized.…We can only guess at the source of this behavior…."

Our deacon candidates discussed pastor-deacon relationships at a theological-reflection group meeting. The guest priest described his relationship with the three deacon candidates of his parish. He sees so much work to be done—feeding the hungry, counseling those who need encouragement, teaching those who have faith questions—and not enough people to do it. He opened all ministries to the deacons at the meeting and offered to accept other candidates having a hard time finding the right parish. One of the candidates responded to the priest's offer and now has an open invitation to participate whenever his schedule and that of the church's intersect.

Conversely, another candidate told of a priest who had refused to make such offers, saying he didn't want his parish to become a deacon-holding place like a parking garage or stable.

One priestly practice that varies is that of liturgical oversight of homily preparation. Some pastors want to be engaged in the deacon candidate's homily preparations as an instructional collaborative process, while others give their deacon candidate full control. Some priests share their own homily preparations with the deacons.

I spoke with a priest about occasional discord between deacons and parish pastors. Why are deacons kept out of the priestly circle of influence, held at arm's length from making a real impact in some parishes?

The priest said, "There is a flaw in the priest-formation process, whereby priests are not formed for the deacon's presence." In essence, priests have lost their sense of community. In the past, three or four priests lived together in community, in a rectory, sometimes with a household staff. If one priest got sick or went on vacation, a substitute was readily available. The give and take left each person supported and aware of the communal living and working arrangements. Currently, many priests have a bachelor mentality, living alone, frequently eating alone, and maintaining the privacy of their lives, responsible for just themselves. When a deacon disrupts the privacy and singleness of the priest's domain, tension can result.

Pastors' relationships to deacon candidates and their wives and families are, like all relationships, based on trust and mutual appreciation. The following behaviors may be helpful in establishing and keeping the relationships healthy:

- Acknowledge that the deacon candidate will take a vow of obedience to the bishop who confers the sacrament of holy orders; pastor-deacon relationships will require tact, diplomacy, understanding, and communication skills.

- Establish trust and accountability early in the relationship with consistent and frequent communication between all parties.

- Discuss realistic expectations and limitations regarding time and availability, and be direct.

- Negotiate for win-win solutions so that the needs of the deacon candidate, his family, and the needs of the parish are addressed.

*She reaches mightily from one end of the earth
    to the other,
and she orders all things well.
I loved her and sought her from my youth;
I desired to take her for my bride,
and became enamored of her beauty.*

THE WISDOM OF SOLOMON 8:1-2

TIME MANAGEMENT

Maria Thompson MacLaughlin

Nothing spells self-sabotage more effectively than the absence of time management. Long before the deacon-formation group began, our family had been actively involved in using time-management techniques. We needed a clear understanding of our daily schedules and events to achieve our long-term goals, so everyone kept a personal calendar, and we met weekly as a family to go over our calendars and resolve scheduling conflicts ahead of time.

Creating a combined schedule for our family was the easiest part of managing our time. *Living* the schedule was another matter. Classes, courses, papers, and exams required a great deal of personal and household organization, so we redesigned a household space for my husband's study and work time.

One of the realities of the deacon program was the increased demand on personal time—something Matthew and I knew from the onset. I made certain that I supported him as much as possible in his endeavor. Negativity on my part would thwart any enthusiasm he felt for the diaconate. I remembered that the wife's role in the deacon program was extremely critical because the husband's success hinged on cooperation and support.

Our family soon learned that a huge component of time management was learning how to say no. There were numerous opportunities to use up time. Community involvements ate up many hours for us as individuals. We quickly learned that instead of accepting a chairmanship, we could help out with a committee. Instead of volunteering to host an event, we could provide support by bringing food. In lieu of attending a meeting, we could have a friend fill us in on highlights.

For Matthew and me, the four deacon-formation years were time-consuming and hectic, so we prioritized our weekends. We used our calendars to block off a weekend whenever we felt we could get away as a couple. In many instances a portion of the weekend was spent proofreading a paper or working on an exam, but the time away was uplifting. After Matthew was ordained it became even more difficult to get away together because of homily preparation or church events. However, we found that going somewhere together was a sort of renewal that equipped us to deal with the rigors of deacon responsibilities.

Time management should include the most important activity of all—prayer. Praying together as a couple is a beautiful and moving experience. Individual prayer is a rejuvenating experience that should be renewed daily. Make time for and keep God foremost in your schedule. After all, your time is really God's time.

An Ending and a Beginning

*May God grant me to speak with judgment,
and to have thoughts worthy of what
    I have received;
for he is the guide even of wisdom
and the corrector of the wise.
For both we and our words are in his hand,
as are all understanding and skill in crafts.
For it is he who gave me unerring knowledge
    of what exists,
to know the structure of the world and the
    activity of the elements…*

THE WISDOM OF SOLOMON 7:15-17

LIFESTYLE CHANGES

Karen A. Harmeyer

Toward the end of the four-year deacon-formation process, the wives met as a group to discuss issues and feelings. The sessions, usually facilitated by one or two female church staff members or candidates' wives, were extremely productive and allowed us to prepare ourselves for situations we'd never encountered before.

Appearance and Behavior

One of the wives mentioned the importance of appropriate dress, especially when meeting with parishioners. Leisure outfits and athletic gear do not present the image of propriety that clergy-parishioner relationships call for. The same concept may be applied to speech patterns, selection of meeting place, and agenda. When visiting ill or hospitalized parishioners, appropriate dress will enhance their response to ministerial offers of comfort, concern, and prayer. Just seeing the deacon in clerical dress may make them feel better.

Another discussion involved protecting the deacon

from the inappropriate advances of parish members. Some wives felt the need to protect their husbands from needy parishioners, and there was concern that some deacons might unknowingly and unconsciously invite such attentions. Marriage is a trust relationship between husband and wife, and part of that relationship includes creating an environment in which trust is maintained while the deacon ministers to others.

When a significant emotional event, such as an unexpected death or tragedy, has occurred, or when one person feels strongly attracted to another and is intent on acting on that impulse, the people involved may be distraught, incapable of rational thought, and unable to make good decisions. In such situations, the person may be a danger to himself or herself and others. How do you respond effectively to that person without aggravating their emotional state and still provide comfort and solace?

Before and after Mass, people run to speak with church officials about family members and friends. Although these discussions could take place by telephone or e-mail, face-to-face interaction creates the more personal connection preferred by many people. The importance of a slight touch of the hand, brief eye contact, or a hug to communicate genuine concern and caring cannot be underestimated. The ministry exists in the touch, concern, and connection. The intimacy of the moment is essential. But sometimes parishioners may be emotionally vulnerable to the caring ministrations they actively seek, and everyday kindnesses may be interpreted as overtures for a closer connection.

The deacon, taking ministry concerns seriously, may be flattered by the attention. How can he be protected from others and from himself?

One wife said that her husband, who was considered attractive by other women, wanted her to screen his telephone calls and direct only certain inquiries to him. She was expressing the threat that others in the room were thinking about but not verbalizing.

Our discussion on this topic led to the formation of these precautionary measures:

- Be sensitive to vulnerable situations.

- Meet people in a formal setting, ideally at the church or in office spaces where other people are present, and dress appropriately.

- Privacy is important, but a door with a window is preferable to a solid door to protect all parties from unfounded allegations of improper behavior.

- Stand beside your husband when in a public gathering. Be visible as his wife so that others can see a close marriage impervious to outside influences and sabotage.

- Establish meeting agendas early and stay focused on that agenda.

- Have an attendant available when a high-risk situation is anticipated.

- Know your church population and the customers of that population; cultures vary regarding the meaning of behaviors like touch and eye contact.

- Install an answering machine with a recording device on your home phone for use when high-risk communications are anticipated.

- Encourage the deacon to be alert when making home visits; he should let others know his schedule.

- Hire an image consultant if your speech, appearance, or demeanor need improving.

- Arrange high-risk communication training as a continuing-education opportunity for the parish staff.

IN THE PUBLIC EYE

The clerical collar and deacon title add a new dimension to public behavior. The reason for a rigorous formation process is to have an informed deacon population that is fluent in Church doctrine and practices. A deacon is a church leader, and therefore his presence at an event or comments on an issue may be seen as official Church position on the issue. Gary and I learned this the hard way when some church volunteers asked him to attend an event and he agreed to do so without knowing exactly what the event was about. When he asked me to go with him to Mass, neither of us knew we were actually attending a political rally, something that, as a military officer, I've been trained to avoid. Because of Gary's deacon status, we had to wait for a pause in the program to make our exit. Although this was a minor controversial justice situation, Gary and I were there. Our error was lack of research regarding what type of event we were attending and what the planned agenda was. We didn't attend in response to a specific issue, we just went. Poor plan.

Here is the plan we will follow in the future:

- Find out who, what, when, where, and the focus of the gathering ahead of time, even when it meets in a church.

- Determine prior to attending how participatory you intend to be.

- Research justice issues prior to engaging in debate regarding the issue.

- When speaking, clearly state whether you are speaking as a citizen or as a Church representative and, if so, under whose authority.

- Recognize that as a deacon or deacon's wife you represent more than yourself because of your position and its recognizable visibility.

- Know that presence alone lends itself to weighing in on an issue, either way.

- If you are averse to controversy, don't go to the event. Show your support or nonsupport in the voting booth.

*As a child I was naturally gifted,
and a good soul fell to my lot;
or rather, being good, I entered an undefiled
  body.
But I perceived that I would not possess wisdom
  unless God gave her to me—
and it was a mark of insight to know whose
  gift she was—
so I appealed to the Lord and implored him…*

THE WISDOM OF SOLOMON 8:19-21

ORDINATION

Karen A. Harmeyer

The gravity of Gary's upcoming ordination hit me like a lightning bolt when I had to sign a preordination document affirming that I agreed to his decision to be ordained and that I was aware that he would not be allowed to remarry except with papal dispensation. Such dispensation is given only under extreme circumstances, for example, if the deacon is widowed with small children who need love and nurturing from a woman as well as a man.

When faced with the decision to become ordained, the vow whereby the deacon candidate agrees not to marry if he is single and not to remarry if he is currently married is a serious one that must be made carefully:

- Discuss the decision openly, lovingly, and honestly.

- Explore the potential impact of the vow on family members to help them understand the consequences of the agreement.

- If you are unable to make an informed decision, delay ordination.

As ordination drew near, the flurry of activity increased in all the deacon-candidate households. The to-do list looked much like plans for an elaborate wedding: select the invitations, plan receptions, and arrange lodging for out-of-town guests. Although the men made many of the planning decisions, their wives were an integral part of the process.

Our group was so large that the deacons were divided into three ordination groups. The churches selected had to be large enough to accommodate the number of family members and guests who would be attending, and the space in front of the altar needed to be big enough for the candidates to lie face down (prostrate) before the bishop as the choir sang or chanted the Litany of the Saints.

The first ordination site was planned at Holy Cross Catholic Church in Lynchburg, representing the Western Vicariate. The second ordination was scheduled a week later at the Cathedral of the Sacred Heart in Richmond, the Central Vicariate. Finally, the third ordination ceremony was set a month later at St. Gregory the Great Catholic Church in Virginia Beach, the Eastern Vicariate. The Most Reverend Walter F. Sullivan, D.D., Bishop of Richmond, was the presider at all three events. Ten men received holy orders as deacons in Lynchburg, twenty in Richmond, and eighteen in Virginia Beach.

Our large group of deacons-in-the-making and wives supported each other through the preordination,

ordination, and postordination periods. We affirmed each others' decisions and applauded this hallmark on the diaconate journey. We all traveled to all three ordinations. We prayed for each other and our ministries. Each person became part of the following statement of our gratitude and determination to serve, which appeared on the ordination program at the three sites.

RICHMOND PERMANENT DIACONATE
STATEMENT FOR ORDINATION

As we celebrate the sacrament of ordination, we humbly seek the continued prayers of the people of the Diocese of Richmond in support of our ministry of word, sacrament, and service. Throughout our time of formation, we have felt the call of the Spirit; the support of our families, friends, and parish communities; and the encouragement of our bishop, priests, religious women and men, brother deacons, and the many lay professionals from our diocesan and parish staffs. We are especially grateful to the Deacon Formation Board and the Benedictine Community of Saint Meinrad for their enthusiasm and wisdom given and shared as part of our formation process. To the people of Saint Michael's Parish, Glen Allen, we give special thanks for their hospitality and prayerful support of this ministry.

We know well that our formation is incomplete and ongoing. We are mindful of the many issues of justice that are yet to be addressed in our communities, our world, and our Church. We pray for hearts and minds that will be filled with compassion and always open to the Spirit as we live out this sacrament together in the future. We recognize that the ministries of service to which we have been called are many and varied. We recognize with certainty that we will need the support of all people of faith in our diocese to guide us in these new tasks.

As we go from this time and place, we look forward with hope that our shared ministry may become meaningful in service to the people of God throughout our diocese. We pray that our ministries may be united in faith and hope and in collaboration with all of the diocesan and parish professional ministers and with those who have led us so well for so long—our bishop, priests, religious, and deacons who together have brought us "*this far by faith.*" We thank God for the gift of this sacrament in our lives. We thank all of you for your faith and your support of this ministry.

Peace and Blessings,
The Richmond Diaconate Community

Gary was ordained a permanent deacon at the Virginia Beach site. Protestors toted placards and banners showing their disapproval that the diaconate was not open to women. Although quietly obvious, they did not disrupt the events of the day.

I placed the stole over Gary's head, positioned it on his left shoulder, draped it across his chest like a sash, aligned the connection just below his right hip, and finally let it fall freely after the junction. What went through my mind and heart as I touched my husband in his pressed white alb, draped with a fine fabric white stole, shining with the luminescence of the Holy Spirit? My deacon! What a powerful, emotional moment!

Gary's father received the Blood of Christ for the first time from his son, the deacon. Our mothers, siblings, and other family members shed tears of joy with him. Our children celebrated their father's choice to reinvent himself in this manner by following the call that he chose to answer.

We love and support him totally.

For everything there is a season,
and a time for every matter under heaven:
a time to be born, and a time to die;
a time to plant, and a time to pluck up
    what is planted;
a time to kill, and a time to heal;
a time to break down, and a time to build up;
a time to weep, and a time to laugh;
a time to mourn, and a time to dance;
a time to throw away stones, and a time to
    gather stones together;
a time to embrace, and a time to refrain
from embracing;
a time to seek, and a time to lose;
a time to keep, and a time to throw away;
a time to tear, and a time to sew;
a time to keep silence, and a time to speak;
a time to love, and a time to hate;
a time for war, and a time for peace.

ECCLESIASTES 3:1-8

A NEW LIFE

Karen A. Harmeyer

By the time of the final weekend of the formation process, most of the deacons had been ordained. When we gathered for the evening prayer service, the couples seemed more reverent than usual. This final weekend together meant saying goodbye to the discernment and formal formation process. When the opening hymn began, a truly joyful sound rose to the rafters of St. Michael's Church. It was as though a new level of confidence and self-assurance emitted from all present. The Holy Spirit found new brilliance in its vessels that night. We would all remember our unity with each other, our shared journey, and our new challenges to serve others every day of our lives.

Six months after ordination, the couples gathered to assess progress and challenges, critique the program, and focus on improving the formation process for future deacon candidates.

Accomplishments

- Full involvement in parish ministries, including liturgical duties, sacramental preparation and administration, religious education and development, numerous outreach activities, and various justice and peace interactions.

- Perceived as integral in forming small faith groups in select parishes, an activity in which the group anticipated increased involvement and growth over time.

- Engagement in numerous ministry-to-the-sick functions, providing comfort and spiritual bolstering to the chronic and terminally ill, nurturing to the caregivers who tend them, and directing congregation members who visit the sick in hospitals, nursing facilities, and private homes.

- Successful transition from parish staff member to ministry leader and parish leader.

- Improved preaching at the churches because of the varied methods, research efforts, and creative delivery skills made possible by having rotating homilists (priests and deacons).

- Officiating at sacraments and sacramental preparations. Some deacons experienced heightened involvement and familial gratification when officiating at family members' baptisms, first Eucharists, and weddings.

- Encouraging and empowering lay ministers in their ministry efforts through teamwork and emphasis on creating an environment of trust, cooperation, and shared vision and mission. The deacons and their wives perceived creating and building ministry teams as critical leadership skills to be used often.

- Being highly useful: "Everyone wants us to do something."

- Keeping theological-reflection groups functioning, thus providing a forum for open discussion of issues, continuing-education opportunities, and evaluation of needs, while realizing mutual growth through the small-group experience.

- Having received twelve hours of master's level credit for the diocese's diaconate program, several deacons were well on their way to a master's degree in pastoral theology.

Disappointments

- At the initial information sessions, the sales pitch mentioned the possibility of a master's degree at the end of formation. It would be one way to give the program a recognized level of credibility, and clergy and other professionals would accept the recognized standard. However, changes in instructors occurred, the rigor declined, and the academic challenge to the deacon students and their wives declined. It became clear that there would be no master's degree for either the deacons or their wives at the end of the program.

- For some of the wives, the opportunity to acquire the master's degree was a factor in their support of the program. If the wives had not been encouraged to commit to the academic portion of formation, we would have had the time to bond more tightly and discover more about each other as individuals and as a group as we centered on preparing for our new role and exploring greater group-cohesiveness benefits.

- Without the enticement of the degree and being taken seriously, attendance did not carry the importance it did initially, and wives were absent on deacon weekends in greater numbers as the four-year program progressed.

Challenges

- Although deacons are encouraged to minister to the sick, they cannot anoint them. Having limited sacramental powers sometimes creates an uncomfortable situation.

- Continuing education must be structured and monitored at the diocesan level. Keeping abreast of current Church teachings, modifications in practice, and leadership direction will be an ongoing challenge.

- The delicate balance between the diaconate role and other life roles such as job position, parent, marriage partner, and volunteer is a dynamic reality of life subject to daily recalibration by the individuals, family members, employers, and parish leadership and congregations.

- Accepting the public nature of clericalism. Each deacon and his wife are now public figures with public scrutiny and ownership applied to every move and motion; public property allows public oversight, expectations, and interpretations. We must live the image.

- Because parishioners who are informed consumers of the diaconate gifts will help ensure the value of the diaconate program, there is an ongoing need to teach about the diaconate, especially with respect to vocation inquiries and development.

- Deacon migration—deacons moving from parish to parish. Some deacons and their wives are still seeking the right fit.

- The biggest gift of the diaconate program has been the opportunity to experience and grow with some of the most amazing men and women anywhere. The deacon couples bring God's love to all they touch. God bless them.

Epilogue

Today, as I listen to Gary's homily, I feel the congregation respond to his simple message of how, in a marriage, the partners make a conscious decision to love each other, the choice seeming to make a mature partnership nobler:

> The women the deacons chose to marry are absolutely gifted. Cherish them. Keep them close to your heart. Know that they love those they serve. They flourish in their role beside, and in addition to, the deacon's ministry efforts. Most of all, these women are individuals in their own right, with talents and foibles unique to each person. God bless them and those they serve.

Gary is sharing his humanness in ministry to others. As he shares stories of our journey of love decisions, I unleash my privacy barriers and let them gently escape, like dark shadows faded by morning light. Members of the congregation are sending Gary feedback as they experience similar warmth and release. The intimacy of the message has an inspired power beyond words.

The parish priest exclaimed as Gary finished, "When I hear our deacons share parts of their lives with us, I wonder if we should let their wives speak, also?" After Mass, I asked, "Father, I'm certain I heard you extend an invitation to me to speak at the ambo. Did I hear you correctly?" Without blinking, he said, "I did." Little does he realize that many of Gary's words were composed through the unspoken language of our shared life.

Spouses frequently speak without words simply by being a part of each others' lives. Our message is one of togetherness. This book documents a small part of the transformation experienced by partners in the process.

Karen A. Harmeyer

ADDITIONAL RESOURCES

Deacon Digest
Alt Publishing Co.
502 George Street
De Pere, WI 54115
www.deacondigest.com

Deacon's Place
www.deaconsplace.info

National Assocation of Deacon Organizations
www.nado.us

National Association of Diaconate Directors
2136 12th Street, Suite 105
Rockford, IL 61104
www.nadd.cc

National Diaconate Institute for Continuing Education
www.ndice.org

United States Conference of Catholic Bishops
Secretariat for the Diaconate
3211 4th Street, NE
Washington, DC 20017-1194
www.usccb.org/deacon

ABOUT THE AUTHORS

Karen A. Harmeyer is a retired United States Naval Reserve rear admiral. She holds a Bachelor of Science in Nursing from the University of Iowa and a Master of Arts in Management from Webster University. She and her husband, Deacon Gary Harmeyer, live in Virginia Beach, Virginia.

Maria Thompson MacLaughlin has been a teacher for twenty-five years. She holds a Bachelor of Science in Elementary Education from Longwood College and a Master of Education in Educational Administration and Supervision from Virginia State University. She and her husband, Deacon Matthew MacLaughlin, live in Petersburg, Virginia.